THE CASH FLOW CHALLENGE

The Cash Flow Challenge

Philip Ramsden

Gower

Published by
Gower Publishing Limited
Gower House
Croft Road
Aldershot
Hampshire GU11 3HR
England

Gower
Old Post Road
Brookfield
Vermont 05036
USA

Philip Ramsden has asserted his right under the Copyright, Designs and Patents Act 1988 to be identified as the author of this work.

British Library Cataloguing in Publication Data
Ramsden, Philip
    The cash flow challenge
    1. Cash flow 2. Cash management
    I. Title
    658.1′52′44

ISBN 0 566 07807 4
Typeset in Plantin by Intype London Ltd
and printed in Great Britain by Biddles Ltd, Guildford.

Contents

Preface

Role playing is a safe way to gain experience. It has the added advantage that if you don't get the job done first time, you can have another go and learn from your mistakes.

Written in an informal and entertaining style, this book challenges you to take the part of a Financial Director of a fictitious multi-million pound company, who is given a cash flow target to achieve.

In accepting the challenge you will learn how cash flow, vitally important to any organization, is controlled. It is a subject essential to every manager in any function or discipline – everyone spends money!

No accounting experience is necessary. You're ready now to be the Financial Director of Daisy House Limited, whether you're really in Personnel, Sales, R&D, Production, Purchasing, Computing or anywhere – even in Accounts or the Managing Director.

Philip Ramsden

About the IFA

The Institute of Financial Accountants was founded in 1916 as the Institute of Book-keepers. The objective was to offer a professional qualification to the person who was primarily responsible for the in-house accounting and worked in what was then called the Counting House. To reflect the changes and the improved status of its members the Institute changed its name several times and became the Institute of Financial Accountants on 23rd December 1987.

The Institute is now the largest of the non-chartered body of accountants offering a professional accountancy qualification which is highly respected, with members working in industry and commerce, local government and public practice.

The Institute offers two grades of membership; Associate and Fellow. Membership may be achieved by passing the Institute's professional examination through exemption by passing an equivalent examination, or by accreditation of prior learning (APL) which is a test of a person's competence in the workplace by a qualified assessor.

The examination structure of the Institute is in four parts with fourteen subjects, which has been constantly updated on a regular basis to reflect the changes and demands required of an Accountant. Exemptions are granted to holders of HNC/HND in Business and Finance, which include the management accounting and financial accounting modules, business and accounting degrees and parts of other recognised accountancy qualifications.

Introduction

The control of cash within an organization is extremely important. Even if a company is profitable, if it does not have sufficient cash to pay its way, suppliers will cease to provide the goods and services the company requires to produce its own wares. Profit can be measured simply by total sales less all costs. This will invariably differ from the cash amount that the company has.

The cash flow is affected by how long you give customers to pay you after a sale; how long creditors will wait before you pay them; the timing (and size) of other payments such as wages and salaries, VAT, dividends, bank interest and so on.

Arguments rage in the accounting profession as to how cash flow, which is the change in the company's cash position, should best be measured. At the most simple level, it could be the change in the company's bank account (or overdraft). Management of the cash flow tends to work on the basis that, if all other elements of the balance sheet are well managed, the cash figure will automatically follow. Hence the emphasis tends to be on collecting cash from customers and being judicious in parting with cash to anyone else.

It is also important to bear in mind the relevant timeframe. Early in a company's life, cash is king. Without a trading history it is difficult to obtain credit from suppliers. On the other hand, customers will usually be expecting to buy on credit terms. A net outflow of cash is common in these circumstances and, in its early days, the company may have to borrow until it can demonstrate its likely survival to suppliers and receive goods and services on credit.

Even with established companies, there can be occasional large calls on cash – for example, the payments of dividends or corporation tax can be for considerable amounts which must be settled in cash at the appropriate time. Events such as these can be planned for, but circumstances can arise where management skill is required to effectively deal with unexpected opportunities or threats.

The following Challenge is a business scenario game. To play it, you will need a pencil to record your progress in dealing with the events that arise. You may wish to study 'A Guide to Cash Flow Control' (pp. 137–41) before you start if you think you need some initial guidance. Or you can just get on with the Challenge.

Setting the Scene

Daisy House Limited

As the Financial Director of Daisy House Limited, you will be presented with a number of decisions that may help or hinder you in your mission. Since actions have consequences, at some point you will receive a score. There are two types of score in this challenge:

- £s – in or out of the company;
- Business Points – reflecting the 'style' with which you made your decisions.

Your decisions will gain (or lose) you £s and Business Points. Sometimes the 'right' decision will gain you £s but lose you Business Points and vice versa. In reality, business practice contains many grey areas of 'right' and 'wrong'.

As you work through the Challenge, note your £ scores and Business Points given (together with

the reason – for example, 'Bank') at the appropriate point. A score sheet is given on page 143.
And so . . . to the office!

Background and objective

Daisy House Limited is the largest operating division of an established major UK company. The senior management team is as follows:

- Derek – Managing Director
- You – Finance Director
- Louise – Production Director
- Claire – Sales Director.

The key people within your Finance department are:

- John – Financial Controller
- Shirley – Credit Controller
- Bob – Purchase Ledger Supervisor

Unfortunately John is away on honeymoon in Kenya for the next month.

On Monday morning, as you walk into your office, the telephone rings. It is Sheila, the Group Financial Director based at Head Office. She tells you that the Group has identified a sudden opportunity to make an excellent strategic acquisition of a small competitor, but they will have to be quick. Of the proposed purchase price, half can be borrowed from the company's bank if the Group can find the other half. All the companies in the Group will have to help and Sheila has decided that your company should contribute a positive cash flow of £1 million – in the next month.

Sheila does point out that she realizes that, in order to achieve this, you will probably be bringing forward cash flow from future months into this month and will consequently have a lower cash flow in the future. However, she adds that the Group needs good cash flow figures to show the bank and that the company to be acquired has considerable liquid assets which will sustain the Group over that time. You need not worry about this aspect – you just have to find that £1 million.

After the call, you review the cash forecast which John left for you before he went away. It is in a standard format:

	Next month's cash forecast
	£
Profit after tax	205 000
Add back depreciation	14 000
Cash flow from operations	229 000
Change in:	
Debtors	68 000 (increase)
Stocks	80 000 (increase)
Creditors	(54 000) (increase)
Net change in working capital	94 000
Fixed asset expenditure	–
Net change in cash position	135 000 (increase)

This is what you would have expected your cash flow to be under normal operating conditions. By managing it more effectively, you can increase it significantly in the short term – so you have a target of finding an extra £865 000 by the end of the month. Good luck!

The Challenge

1

On your way in, this morning, you see Derek, your MD, in his office. Do you want to talk to him?

(a) Yes. Go to **46**.

(b) No. Go to **30**.

2

You give Derek the background information. He is irritated. 'You should have brought this up earlier. It looks like ToyBoyz are in a right jam. They've been giving us the runaround for some time and it seems that it all could have been easily avoided.'

You look at him puzzled – what does he mean? Go to **81**.

3

Honesty and business integrity are not yet dead! You've not saved any money by paying this group of creditors, but you've avoided tarnishing your company's reputation.

Score: 2nd Creditors £nil; Business Points +5. Go to **139**.

4

With a look of disapproval at being forced to tell a white lie, Shirley tells the man that you are not in the office today. She promises to pass on his information and hangs up. Do you

(a) move on to the next customer? Go to **204**.

(b) backtrack to the Eggy file to see what the problem might be? Go to **240**.

5

You fax your result to the Group Financial Director. It was never an easy task to achieve in such a short time and, although you achieved well above the normal cash flow for the month, it was not enough for the Group's requirements. Although other Financial Directors in the group performed reasonably well, your shortfall was too large for them to make up and the acquisition fell through. Go to **194**.

6

She is happy to do so. 'No money and you will go on stop. It would be a serious blow to the longstanding business relationship between our two companies.'

Do you

(a) take the hint at last and pay? Go to **127**.

(b) stand your ground – you can afford to do without them more than they can do without you – and, after all, you are the customer! Go to **89**.

7

Claire reads from the order book. 'Tinklebell – one Whizzo Multiplexer, delivery within three months, price £35 000. Standard terms and conditions.' Before you can ask, she adds, 'That means 30 days' credit terms. Shall I sell it to them instead? It will mean lower sales and less profit this month than if I sell it to Hajid.'

Do you

(a)   agree to sell it to Hajid? Go to **75**.

(b)   prefer to sell it to Tinklebell? Go to **245**.

8

When you explain the full details of the outstanding debt to Barry, he agrees that you have a problem: £166 000 is far more than Synbad would normally owe Atled. He would like to help.

Do you

(a)   accept his offer to deal with it when he visits Synbad in six weeks' time? Go to **155**.

(b)   decline his offer and ask Shirley to send a fax in your name to Synbad, demanding immediate payment? Go to **85**.

(c)   ask Barry if he can put any pressure on Synbad himself? Go to **247**.

(d)   decide that it's all getting too complicated

and leave this one for Shirley to chase? Go to **120**.

9

Bob is adamant that the VAT office will notice the late payment. 'They're very hot on this sort of thing because we actually get a credit extension anyway. However, if we are a couple of days late, we are more likely to get a warning than a fine as this would be the first time that we've been late. It's simple enough to blame administrative problems or absence of key personnel or authorized signatories, but there's no guarantee that we won't get fined. It's your decision.'

Do you tell Bob

(a)   to go ahead and pay on time. Go to **223**.

(b)   that you've reconsidered and have decided it should be paid on time, but would like to know if there's a way to reduce the amount? Go to **108**.

(c)   that you will take full responsibility and that he is to pay the VAT on the first Monday after the cash deadline. Go to **153**.

10

He tells you that his head office has already informed him of the situations, since it is his bank that is funding the other half of the acquisition. He therefore cannot help you; the Group must find the other half.

Well, you've gained no money, but at least you were honest.

Score: Bank £nil; Business Points +1. Go to 146.

11

Go to 118.

12

'I'm afraid that I can't do that,' Mr Adale replies. 'I've just paid the quarterly VAT and the income tax and national insurance contributions and there's not enough cash in our account to cover the transfer unless this incoming payment clears today. Are you sure that you won't accept a cheque dated Monday? I'll send it by first-class post.'

Do you

(a) reluctantly accept the cheque? Go to **196**.

(b) try to argue for another solution? Go to **210**.

13

Mr Andrews' response is terse and to the point: 'I can't tell you one way or the other – that would be breaking confidentiality. Goodbye.' Go to **115**.

14

Big mistake! The following week, Ammag's Financial Director sends you a memo pointing out your overdue intercompany debt – and it is copied to the Group Financial Director. Go to **98**.

15

By the end of the following week, nothing has been received from ToyBoyz. Shirley has rung often but is always told that Mr Adale is out of the office that day and will be away on business all week. Apparently only Mr Adale or the MD at ToyBoyz can deal with the matter.

Do you

(a) ring the MD of ToyBoyz? Go to **149**.

(b) wait for Mr Adale to return? Go to **96**.

(c) leave this to Shirley from now on? Go to **59**.

(d) speak you your MD? Go to **2**.

(e) ring the ToyBoyz Production Manager? Go to **186**.

16

Shirley reports that the woman at Essayess was offended at the idea, interpreting this as meaning that you did not trust them to pay on time. Even so, they have agreed to have a cheque ready for collection. As it happens, one of your salespeople will be in the area and will be able to pick up the cheque.

Do you

(a) arrange with Claire for the sales representative to pick up the cheque? Go to **177**.

(b) ring the MD at Essayess to explain why

you want to collect the cheque? Go to **212**.

17

After a few more seconds you are put through. An aggressive voice hits you . . . 'This is Allan Adale, Financial Director, I understand that you threatened my receptionist with legal action if she did not interrupt my very important meeting with a customer.'

Do you

- (a) apologize and offer to speak again at a more convenient time? Go to **24**.

- (b) counter his obvious aggression by telling him forthrightly that if you do not get a cheque for £220 000 tomorrow, you will have ToyBoyz liquidated? Go to **137**.

- (c) point out calmly that the legal action is not against the receptionist, but will be against ToyBoyz unless you and he can resolve the issue of an outstanding payment of £220 000? Go to **253**.

18

The deal is struck. By the end of the week Essayess have a Model B Gantry system and you have a cheque.

Score: Essayess +£19 800; Business Points +1. Go to **201**.

19

This is nothing less than cheating HM Customs and Excise.

Score: VAT +£148 000; Business Points −10. Go to **142**.

20

The following day you get a memo from the Sales Director, Claire, copied to the MD and the warehouse manager.

'It appears that you have raised a credit note for £8000 to Triller. Although you have the authority to do so, this amount is deducted from *my* sales performance and I approve all credit notes first. Furthermore, it appears that the credit note is not warranted because the goods left here in good condition. It is too late to do anything about it now, but please do not do this again without reference to me.'

Derek, your MD, calls you to his office. Go to **101**.

21

Claire beams radiantly at you. 'I'd like to help you, but this is really more Shirley's area than mine. If she ever has trouble with particular customers, then she keeps me informed, but, really, getting the money in from your customers is your department, not mine. My job stops when the orders come in.'

Do you

(a) agree and change the subject? Return to **249**.

(b) challenge her on the grounds that her involvement is not complete until the customer is satisfied? Go to **61**.

(c) press your case about her responsibility for cash collection? Go to **180**.

22

If more people in business operated in the same way as you, we would not need *Which?* magazine, the Citizens' Advice Bureau or television's *Watchdog*! You play the game straight and true – and people trust you for it.

Of course this may not count for much unless you actually do the job you are paid to do, but they cannot take away the personal satisfaction that comes from doing what is 'right'. Go to **256**.

23

'Creditors? You're the one who pays them, but I'll tell you something for nothing – if you stop paying suppliers and they stop supplying, I will tell the MD whose fault it is that production has stopped.'

Point taken? Louise leaves your office. Go to **184**.

24

Sounding as though he is barely controlling his anger, Mr Adale replies, 'No, you've interrupted me now, you might as well carry on rather than threaten my receptionist again some other time. What is it that you want?'

You explain that you are concerned about the debt of £220 000 which is more than three months overdue. Go to **246**.

25

Next on Bob's list are the payments to the utilities – gas, electric, water, telephones, and so on. As he said, it is unlikely that they will cut you off if you pay straight after the deadline. Do you want to risk it?

(a) No, pay them on time. Go to **192**.

(b) Yes – the worst thing that can happen is that production grinds to a halt! Go to **214**.

26

The month goes by. It is past your deadline, but obviously you are interested in knowing whether you have an imminent bad debt to write off. You took the risk – did it pay off? Sometimes business is about luck as well as skill. Choose a way forward.

(a)   Go to **190**.

(b)   Go to **110**.

(c)   Go to **151**.

(d)   Go to **208**.

27

Mr Adale fails to surface during the week and never returns Shirley's calls. Go to **158**.

28

Claire recalls that the order was placed at the National Exhibition in London. Her counterpart at your sister company, Atled Limited, seemed to know the buyer.

Do you want to

(a)   ring Barry, the Sales Director at Atled? Go to **179**.

(b)   leave this and consider Shirley's other options? Return to **204** and make another choice.

29

Bob tells you, 'Our weekly cheque run for suppliers is between £150 000 and £200 000.' He offers to stop all such payments for the next four weeks, but adds, 'It will create a lot of problems, especially for my department. I can put some of them off if I can promise payment on the first day after the deadline.'

Do you want to

(a) accept Bob's suggestion and not pay anyone? Go to **169**.

(b) ask Bob if he can identify those suppliers who will cause the most problems? Go to **64**.

(c) pay the cheques out as usual? Go to **189**.

30

You could ring the bank manager. Is it likely that he could solve your problems with a simple loan?

Do you

(a) ring him and ask? Go to **106**.

(b) try a different tack? Go to **146**.

31

'A straightforward question for you, Claire. Do you have anything in the order book that we may be able to bring forward?'

Claire summons the senior administrator who brings the order book with him. She glances through it and comes up with some possibilities. Go to **152**.

32

The second cheque arrives – and bounces two days later. You ring Mr Adale and are told that he is unavailable, despite your threat to visit him personally.

Do you

(a)   opt to take legal action? Go to **84**.

(b)   inform your Managing Director? Go to **2**.

(c)   give this one up? Go to **80**.

33

Two days later you get a call from your MD, Derek. 'Come to my office.'

His tone reminds you of the time you were

summoned to the headmaster's office as a third former. When you get there, you face an irate Purchasing Manager and a purple faced Production Director. Go to **148**.

34

Mr Adale continues, 'Unfortunately I have a slight problem. It's an awkward time at the moment to pay such a large amount. That payment I told you about earlier is due in any day now. Can I call you when we have that?'

What is your response?

(a) Yes. Call me on this number? Go to **199**.

(b) 'No, this debt is long overdue and we need to sort out an immediate settlement.' Go to **90**.

35

Despite her persistence, Shirley fails to make contact with Mr Adale that week, nor does he return any of her calls. Go to **100**.

36

You sign the fax and Shirley sends it. Go to **232**.

37

Shirley checks with Tinklebell that there are no problems. She also asks if the cheque could be in your hands by the due date. They agree to post it first class the day before the due date, unless you want to collect it. Unfortunately Tinklebell is 120 miles away and a courier will cost you £100.
  Do you

  (a)   trust the cheque to the post? Go to **174**.

  (b)   send an express rider to collect it? Go to **150**.

38

Thirty seconds later Bob rings back. 'Sorry, but I tried. They insist on going over my head and there's only you.'
  You are sure that Bob did not mean that quite how it sounded, so you put on a brave face and accept the call. Go to **83**.

39

The legal wheels grind into action. The first letter, demanding settlement of the debt within seven days, goes unheeded. The solicitor advises you to sue for the debt, plus interest and costs, in court.

If you lose, costs will be around £6000, but the solicitor is confident of success.

Will you

(a)   proceed to issue a summons? Go to **114**.

(b)   tell your MD what you are proposing to do? Go to **81**.

40

Shirley reports back that Essayess have no objection to the cheque being collected on the due date. A sales representative in the area that day picks up the cheque for you. Making sure the money was in on time was a shrewd move.

Score: Essayess +£20 900; Business Points +1. Go to **201**.

41

Triller give you the same story as Shirley told you. They will not pay unless they receive the credit for £8000. Go to **254**.

42

Good decision. Go to **104**.

43

You have now exhausted all the possibilities for getting the money into the company. Try the other side of the equation with Bob, the Purchase Ledger Supervisor. Go to **217**.

44

Dominic replies, 'I do understand, but it's your problem. I can't afford to subsidize your cash flow at the expense of mine. Either we collect a cheque tomorrow or I will have to back my Credit Controller and put you on stop.'

Do you

(a) pay up? Go to **127**.

(b) accept going on stop? Go to **33**.

45

This is nothing less than cheating HM Customs and Excise.

Score: VAT +£113 000; Business Points −10. Go to **142**.

46

You tell Derek what the Group Financial Director said. He replies, 'We had better cooperate then. You are the financial wizard around here. Do what it takes.'

It looks as though you've been given full responsibility! Go to **30**.

47

'Yes, I have the invoice somewhere, but there are a few problems. We've had some technical difficulties with your Pro-Tem Phase II Sorter/ Developer. Apparently it hasn't been performing to its specification.'

This is news to you (and Shirley) and you tell him so. He replies, 'Rather than involve us both in a lot of administration, blaming each other and sending letters back and forth and so on, we decided that it would be much friendlier if we just tried to fix it ourselves. Of course that means that I can't sanction payment until our Production Manager is happy with the machine's performance.'

You are not going to fall for this story. Do you

(a)   insist on sending your Production Director and Senior Engineer over to sort it out? Go to **73**.

(b)   point out that the machine was delivered nearly six months ago and that it passed through its commissioning phase without any comment from ToyBoyz? Go to **170**.

48

Claire continues, 'The second possibility is an order for a Model B Gantry system, from Essayess in Oldham, £22 000, delivery next month, 30 days' credit. This is a new customer, but the credit terms were agreed after Shirley did the routine checks.'

'What exactly is the possibility with this order?' you ask.

'I can ask them to accept delivery this month instead. We can invoice them and they pay after 30 days,' offers Claire.

You brighten at the suggestion and then realize that without a track record, you don't know whether they will pay on time and you have no leeway with the deadline.

Do you suggest that

(a)   you forget this one? Go to **201**.

(b)   Claire rings Essayess and asks whether they will accept immediate delivery and hope that they pay on time? Go to **143**.

(c)   you offer them a 5 per cent discount if they pay cash on delivery, since they are a new customer after all? Go to **56**.

49

'Hello, this is Jennifer Littlejohn, MD of ToyBoyz. How can I help you?'

You explain the problem of the age of the debt, the promise made by Mr Adale and the absence of any payment.

'It's the first I have heard about this, I'm afraid. There's a big payment due in to us soon, I believe, but I couldn't say quite when. Mr Adale would know the details. I suggest that you wait until he returns.'

Do you

(a) accept her advice? Go to **124**.

(b) ask her if she could authorize payment herself? Go to **166**.

50

There is no easy way to give bad news, so you bite the bullet and telephone the Group Financial Director. As you expect, she is unimpressed by such a poor result from the Financial Director of the main operating division of the group. To make it worse, she tells you that all the other Financial Directors in the Group achieved their targets but, because of your failure, the acquisition will not now take place. Go to **194**.

51

The following day, do you

(a) leave the matter for Shirley to deal with? Go to **43**.

(b) Ring ToyBoyz's Financial Director again? Go to **172**.

52

'The middle group wouldn't be too difficult for us to deal with if we didn't pay them this month,' continues Bob. 'Those due in the last two weeks will get paid at just about the point when they'll be considering chasing us for the money. The suppliers due to be paid in the next two weeks will be writing and ringing during the last two. My people can stall for two weeks, especially in the last week of the month when we can promise a cheque on the following Monday. Delaying payments to this group would save about £260 000.'

What is your decision?

(a) Pay them as normal. Go to **3**.

(b) Delay payment until after the deadline. Go to **211**.

53

That is all you can achieve with the paying out side of the business. Go to **160**.

54

Shirley rings Triller to say that the credit note is on its way. They agree to pay £392 000 by the end of the week. Go to **20**.

55

This is nothing less than defrauding HM Customs and Excise.

Score: VAT +£183 000; Business Points −10. Go to **142**.

56

Claire rings the Managing Director of Essayess. She is trying to persuade him to accept immediate delivery but her expression tells you that she is having no success.

When she proposes a 5 per cent discount if he will also pay cash on delivery, you can hear him explode with fury. Go to **224**.

57

Oh dear! The cheque has bounced! Do you

- (a) re-present it to the bank? Go to **244**.
- (b) ring Mr Adale? Go to **156**.
- (c) bring your MD up-to-date with events? Go to **2**.

58

The leasing company faxes the paperwork over to you. When you work it out, the total payments come to £1 225 000 over the next five years. This is above your authorization limit for leasing contracts and has to be approved by the Group Financial Director. Do you

- (a) ring the leasing company and tell them that you have changed your mind? Go to **206**.
- (b) ring Sheila, the Group Financial Director, and tell her about the proposal? Go to **112**.

59

Nothing happens. Walking away from it isn't likely to make anything happen either.

Score: ToyBoyz £nil, Business Points −1. Go to **43**.

60

He does not ring you back that day. Go to **51**.

61

You counter, 'Surely you need to see the deal through, until the product is delivered to the customer in working order? After all, any comeback goes straight to you, not to Production or the warehouse.'

Claire considers this. 'Agreed, you have a point. However, the collection of cash is still one of your functions, although I'm happy to help Shirley in specific instances.'

You decided to change the subject. Go to **249**.

62

Go to **196**.

63

The file shows that this is your company's first sale to Synbad, and that the 30-day credit term was offered after references from your sister company, Atled Limited. Return to **204** and make another choice.

64

Bob finds that he can readily split the suppliers into three categories:

1. those who scream and shout as soon as the debt is overdue;
2. those who will wait a couple of weeks until after the due date before they begin to chase payment;
3. those who let a month slip by before they even notice that you have not paid them, or at least leave it that long before they take any action.

To save time, Bob asks you if you want to pay

everyone regardless, none of them at all or be selective.

Do you

(a)   pay everyone as usual? Go to **189**.

(b)   pay none of them? Go to **169**.

(c)   be selective, using Bob's criteria? Go to **117**.

65

This is not difficult to work out, since they all ask. The money you thought you had saved disappears again and you seem a little weak to your suppliers.

Score: erase all previous £ scores for

* 1st Creditors
* Onu Oils
* Mystery Metals

and take further Business Points −1. Go to **53**.

66

Lucy passes you on to Dominic, Financial Director of Mystery Metals.

'Dominic, I want to be perfectly honest with you. I've had instructions from Head Office to increase my cash flow over the next month. As much as I dislike doing this, the only way I am going to achieve it is with the help of major suppliers such as yourself. If I can defer payment to you until the first Monday of next month, it will give me a fighting chance. What do you say?'

Does your honesty pay off? Choose from the following:

(a) Go to **222**.

(b) Go to **44**.

(c) Go to **176**.

(d) Go to **71**.

67

By the end of the following week, Shirley has heard nothing. The following Monday she tells you that she has rung ToyBoyz, but Mr Adale will be out of the office on business all week. Apparently only Mr Adale or the Managing

Director at ToyBoyz can deal with this. She has left a message for him to ring back, but, like you, she does not expect too much. Do you

- (a) ring the Managing Director at ToyBoyz? Go to **49**.

- (b) wait for the return of Mr Adale? Go to **124**.

- (c) leave the matter to Shirley from now on? Go to **43**.

- (d) speak to your Managing Director? Go to **2**.

68

It is now the Monday after the deadline. Shirley did very well. She knew that you were under pressure to achieve the target so she and her team put extra effort into making sure that the routine payments were collected on time. She did so well that she brought in more than was forecast.

Start with the base forecast, which was achieved through normal operations:

Base Forecast	+£135 000
add Shirley's efforts	+£35 000
Score: Shirley	+£170 000

Now add/subtract the £ scores you achieved during the month. If your total is

(a)   £900 000 or more, go to **126.**

(b)   between £700 000 and £900 000, go to **200.**

(c)   between £300 000 and £700 000, go to **5.**

(d)   less than £300 000, go to **50.**

69

'Well, fair enough, I'll look into it and pull all the paperwork together. Give me the details and I'll get back to you.' He sounds distinctly unenthusiastic. You give him the details and tell him that you will expect his call that afternoon.

The anticipated call does not materialize, so you telephone him the following day. This time, Mr Adale is ready for you. Go to **47.**

70

The third item on Bob's list is the £43 000 you owe your sister company Ammag. Bob reminds you of the doctrine from the Group Accounting manual: 'You must render any monies due to another Group company upon the appointed day or inform the Group Financial Director in writing in advance if there is any good reason why not.'

Paying Ammag now will help their cash flow at the expense of yours. The payment is due at the end of this week. Will you pay it?

(a) Yes. Go to **175**.

(b) No. Go to **14**.

71

'I've been in the same situation myself in the past', confides Dominic, 'but this an awfully large sum for me to put to one side for so long. I suggest that you pay me half now and the rest on that Monday. Fair enough?'

Can you agree to this proposal?

(a) No, you do not want to pay him anything. Go to **145**.

(b) Yes, it seems a good idea. Go to **235**.

72

Current interest rates are 10 per cent. In exchange for a lump sum of £865 000 (and title to plant and machinery to that value), the leasing company want you to pay £71.10 per quarter per £1000, with the first two payments up front followed by 18 further payments. There is no room for negotiation. Do you want them to send you a contract?

(a)   Yes, you'll have a look at it. Go to **58**.

(b)   No, you decline the offer. Go to **220**.

73

You have called his bluff. Mr Adale sounds a little flustered.

'Really, there's no need – there's probably nothing they could do to help us. Let's stick to the matter of paying you.'

You like this turn in the conversation! Go to **34**.

74

Mr Adale understands your position and faxes you last year's statutory accounts and the company's latest internal accounts. You agree that the latter are to be treated as strictly private and confidential.

From the statutory accounts you gather ToyBoyz made an after-tax profit of £600 000 on sales of £20 000 000. An interesting note is the debenture given to the bank which offers all the fixed assets of the company as security for a five-year loan.

You compare the balance sheets from the statutory accounts and the internal accounts. Go to **178**.

75

Go to **215**.

76

Sometimes naughty, sometimes nice – nobody is perfect. At times you probably anguished over decisions which you made where you were sure that it would bring the money in, but which were against your conscience. It is not always easy to see which way to jump, but you are the one who has to live with your decisions (except in these circumstances when you can go back and have another go!). Go to **256**.

77

The following day, Bob telephones yet again. 'I've had three suppliers on this morning, all demanding immediate payment. One of them let slip that he has heard that we are in financial trouble. I think things are getting out of hand.'

You agree. Rather than Bob refer all the calls to you, which will prevent you from pursuing other methods of achieving the cash flow target, you agree to

(a) pay all the 1st Creditors' group. Go to **241**.

(b) pay any supplier that rings up for payment, from any of the groups. Go to **228**.

(c) pay any supplier from the 1st Creditors' group, but only if they ask. Go to **65**.

After all the financial reputation of your company could be at stake here.

78

Bob relays your decision to Onu immediately and then comes back to you. 'We're on stop!'

'Have we enough oil to keep going?' you ask.

'I doubt it. They deliver a tankerful once a week.'

Do you

(a) pay Onu. Go to **237**.

(b) go on stop – then it will be a Production problem, not a Finance one! Go to **33**.

79

'Then I'll get back to my work,' says Louise, and she leaves your office. Go to **184**.

80

This has been an expensive lesson. In fact it is quite obvious that this is a difficult account, so you shouldn't just leave it.

Score: ToyBoyz £nil; Business Points −5. Go to **43**.

81

'I know Jennifer, the Managing Director at ToyBoyz. She's an honest sort – I'll give her a ring and find out what is at the bottom of all this.' Derek makes the call straightaway and you listen attentively.

After exchanging greetings and stating the purpose of his call, Derek explains that he has you with him, and Jennifer says that Alan Adale, her Financial Director, is in her office. Blunt as ever, Derek asks her what the problem is. Jennifer admits that because some of their investment plans have been slow to pay off, they have run into some short-term difficulties. If they don't defer paying suppliers for about another month they might go under. She offers £5000 as a token payment, but maintains that the remainder will have to wait. Derek looks to you for advice. Do you

(a) accept the £5000 and see what happens in a month's time? Go to **193**.

(b) agree to defer the whole payment for a month? Go to **26**.

(c) insist on pressing for full payment? Go to **234**.

82

This action amounts to nothing less than defrauding HM Customs and Excise.

Score: VAT +£78 000; Business Points −10. Go to **142**.

83

'Hello, Lucy Lewes, Credit Controller at Mystery Metals. I understand that you're having a problem with preparing a cheque for collection tomorrow.'

You try your first defence: 'It's very unusual for us to have cheques collected – we prefer to post them in the usual way.'

'That may be so, but the debt *is* due tomorrow, so to guarantee that payment is made on time, we don't mind the extra expense of collecting it.'

1–0 to Lucy! Go to **133**.

84

The solicitors prepare the court summons. Three days later they inform you that someone has beaten you to it. Another supplier is suing ToyBoyz for £14 000. Two days later the situation gets worse: ToyBoyz's bank calls in its debenture on ToyBoyz's assets. Even if you won your case, there would be no money there with which to pay you. Go to **80**.

85

You ask Shirley to prepare a fax and give it to you for signature later that morning. Go to **36**.

86

The man at the other end of the line introduces himself as Eddy Eggy, Managing Director of Eggy Limited. He points out, rather irately, that he objects to being harassed for money when you owe him more than he owes you. Go to **157**.

87

Nothing else happens and so, on the Monday after the deadline, all the utilities are paid. You saved the money, although there is some damage to the company's reputation (and by association, yours too).

Score: Utilities +£110 000; Business Points −3. Go to **70**.

88

The bank manager asks you why you need the money. Do you tell him about the Group's acquisition plan?

    (a)   Yes, of course. Go to **10**.

    (b)   No, make something up. Go to **167**.

89

Go to **33**.

90

'My hands are tied,' Mr Adale responds. 'The best I can do is to offer you a postdated cheque for next Monday. I am confident that I will have my customer's money by then.'
Do you share his confidence?

    (a)   Yes, you accept the postdated cheque. Go to **62**.

    (b)   No, you insist on a bank transfer payment today. Go to **141**.

91

Thursday dawns and still no word from Mr Adale. You call him back and he explains, 'I've just been on to the bank. Apparently the money has left the foreign bank and it is either with the London clearing bank or our own bank's head office. I have them working on it right now, but you know what banks are like – it'll be tomorrow before they sort it all out. Tomorrow, definitely.'

You have no choice but to wait. Go to **105**.

92

The order, delivery and invoice are processed. The due date for payment is the last day for your cash flow target and you are hoping that Tinklebell will not be even a few days late. Do you

(a) keep your fingers crossed? Go to **164**.

(b) ask Shirley to ring Tinklebell a few days before the due date? Go to **37**.

93

You are not quite sure what the MD says, but it makes Claire blush. She puts down the telephone. 'He declined our generous offer.'

Nevertheless you have stuck to your principles – you weren't prepared to give too much profit away just to get money in quicker. Besides there are other opportunities.

Score: Essayess £nil; Business Points +1. Go to **201**.

94

Louise sits down opposite you. 'Sorry to interrupt you, Louise, but we have a slight problem with cash flow. Head Office want a quick short-term increase.'

You expand on the background, and then Louise responds.

'I'm not entirely ignorant of financial matters, but what goes into the cash flow that I can help you with?'

Do you tell her she can help with

(a) debtors? Go to **213**.

(b) creditors? Go to **23**.

(c)   stocks? Go to **195**.

(d)   fixed assets? Go to **227**.

(e)   nothing? Go to **79**.

95

You receive a cheque a little over four weeks later, on the day before your deadline! Your tactics were successful.

Score: Synbad +£166 000; Business Points +1. Go to **120**.

96

During the week, awaiting Mr Adale's return, do you

(a)   leave the account on ice? Go to **158**.

(b)   have Shirley ring every day, just in case Mr Adale shows up? Go to **27**.

(c)   inform your MD of the problem? Go to **116**.

97

You've backed yourself into a corner with this one. You pay up the difference between the two accounts.

Score: Eggy Limited −£15 000; Business Points nil. Go to **204**.

98

Twenty minutes after the arrival of the memo the Group Financial Director telephones:

'Pay it.'

In a group situation, there is no benefit in one part raising cash at the expense of another. The group cash situation doesn't change, and it causes conflict and friction.

Score: Ammag £nil; Business Points −3. Go to **122**.

99

'It's a large sum, but I think that I could get them down to 60 days. Would that help?'

'No, we need payment within 30 days,' you explain.

'So let's forget Hajid and look at Tinklebell.' Go to 7.

100

Mr Adale is due back today, so you telephone – and he is there.

'Yes, what can I do for you?' The voice is still surly. You remind him that he was going to pay you over a week ago and point out that nothing has happened.

'Yes, we've had a delay with our customer paying us – there's been a mix-up with the letter of credit at their end. It's nothing major, just an administrative error that will delay it for a few days. I am fully expecting payment during this week. I'll call you when it has arrived.'

What is your response?

(a) 'OK – ring me on this number?' Go to **199**.

(b) 'No, that's good enough. This debt is long overdue and we need to sort out an immediate settlement.' Go to **90**.

101

Derek is satisfied with your explanation that £8000 is a small price to pay to receive the balance immediately. Since your company could not prove delivery in good condition, you would have probably eventually sent a credit note anyway.

Nevertheless you agree that it would have been polite to have informed the Sales Director first and avoided her wrath.

Score: Triller +£392 000; Business Points −1. Go to **119**.

102

In the MD's office, you start to explain. 'We might have a bad debt coming up, I've just been through their accounts. They want to delay paying us £220 000 for another month, but the account is already three months overdue. It looks as though they could be in trouble . . .!'

Before you can give him the whole background, Derek interrupts. 'You're the financial wizard round here, not me. You say that you've seen their figures – and they'll make more sense to you than me. You're in a sufficiently senior position to deal with this yourself. It's your decision.'

You ring Mr Adale back. Do you tell him

(a) 'You have your month'? Go to **26**.

(b) 'We cannot help you any more. The debt is long overdue and I insist on immediate settlement'? Go to **147**.

103

The Gantry system is despatched and invoiced at £20 900. The 30-day credit term means that payment is due on your deadline.

Do you

(a) take a chance that the cheque will turn up in time? Go to **185**.

(b) ask Shirley to ask Essayess if you can arrange for a courier to collect the cheque on the due date? Go to **40**.

104

Common sense, honesty, and perhaps a little fear, prevail. Your decision adds nothing more to your prospects of achieving the cash flow target, but it prevents your company's name being discussed in unfavourable terms.

Score: 1st Creditors £nil, Business Points +5. Go to **53**.

105

Your deadline is approaching and time is running out. You telephone Mr Adale.

'No joy yet, I'm afraid, but I'm so confident that it will come in soon that I can offer you a cheque dated for next Monday. How does that sound?' Do you

(a) insist on a bank transfer payment today? Go to **12**.

(b) accept his offer? Go to **196**.

106

After exchanging pleasantries with your bank manager, you get down to business. Do you

(a) tell him what the Group Financial Director has asked you to do? Go to **10**.

(b) ask him for a short-term loan of £865 000? Go to **88**.

107

Of course business is not entirely a matter of achieving the desired figures. There are also ethics, morality, integrity and honesty to consider and, sometimes, these are in direct conflict with the achievement of targets. Occasionally it is a fine line to tread, but every now and then, the 'right' decision even brings in the numbers too.

Total the number of Business Points you scored during your decision-making. You already know how you did against the cash flow target, but how will the Group Financial Director, your Managing Director, your fellow directors, your staff, your customers and suppliers rate *how* you did your job?

If your Business Points score is

(a) 25 or more, go to **22**.

(b) between 6 and 24, go to **76**.

(c) 5 or less, go to **161**.

108

Bob ponders for a moment.

'As you know, there are only two elements to the VAT payable – the amount we add to our sales invoices, less what we are charged by our suppliers on their invoices. I can push the suppliers' invoices through to make sure that more of them are processed than usual. There's nothing wrong with doing that.'

You nod your consent. It will not save much – about £8000 Bob reckons – but every little helps. Bob continues, 'It's trickier with our sales invoicing. The computer system generates a sales invoice when the despatch notes are entered by the warehouse staff. Depending on how desperate you are, we could delay the entry of the despatch notes on the last day of the VAT quarter, which is the end of this week. In fact we could stop entering them all week – it's up to you.'

'How much would that reduce the VAT payment by?' you ask, purely out of interest.

'About £35 000 for each day's despatch notes not entered.'

'What's the risk?' you wisely enquire.

'We do get an annual VAT audit, as you know. Our next one is due not for this quarter, but for the one after. However, the inspector does check all the returns for the preceding 12 months. I would strongly advise against taking this option.

If we were found out, we'd incur penalties for the underdeclaration of VAT due and possibly suffer much heavier consequences if the VAT inspector thought that it was deliberate. Shall I just make sure that the purchase invoices get through a little quicker or leave some of the sales despatches out of the calculation?'

Do you

(a) accelerate the purchase invoices only? Go to **132**.

(b) take the risk – accelerate the purchase invoices and delay some of the despatch note input? Go to **239**.

109

Persistence pays off. You receive a reply saying that a cheque will be with you within 30 days. Do you

(a) fax back asking for immediate settlement, pointing out that the money is long overdue? Go to **159**.

(b) leave it at that? Go to **95**.

110

ToyBoyz are operating, although they are not yet out of the woods. As a gesture of good faith, Mr Adale pays you £50 000 (by bank transfer!) and promises the balance at the end of the following month. You eventually get that too.

The payment was too late for the acquisition, but your persistence and patience paid off in the long run.

Score: ToyBoyz £nil; Business Points +2. Go to **43**.

111

You ring back Mr Eggy, who confirms Bob's information. He agrees that his debt to you is overdue, apologizes for the misunderstanding and agrees to send you a cheque immediately.

Checking the details not only got the money in, but entitles you to feel pleased with yourself too.

Score: Eggy Limited +£45 000; Business Points +1. Go to **204**.

112

Sheila is appalled at your short-term thinking. The interest rate in the contract is over 16 per cent! 'We're not that desperate. Trade your way to the target!'

She is not happy with your performance so far.

Score: Leasing £nil; Business Points −1. Go to 220.

113

The VAT inspector sends you a copy of his report – he has spotted the delayed despatch notes and is duty bound to report them. Wisely Bob did not put your instructions in writing, and the company's official story is based on administrative oversight, computer failure and unfortunate timing in that it all happened at a VAT quarter end. This is not sufficient to escape a penalty for the underdeclaration, a charge for interest and a severe rebuke from the VAT inspector. The company's good history of record-keeping and prompt payment has warded off any suggestions of deliberate fraud, but the VAT inspector will keep a close eye on your company in the future. Go to 25.

114

The court hearing is set for five weeks' time. Unfortunately, before it takes place, your solicitors inform you that ToyBoyz's bank has called in its debenture on the company's assets. It was worried about the impending court case and pulled the plug on ToyBoyz in order to offset its loan to the company. Effectively, ToyBoyz has gone bankrupt.

The legal recourse was perhaps something of a panic reaction given the hints about ToyBoyz's financial predicament.

Score: ToyBoyz −£3000 (legal costs); Business Points −1. Go to **43**.

115

You telephone Mr Adale again. He offers you yet another cheque. Do you accept?

(a)   Yes. Go to **32**.

(b)   No. Go to **242**.

116

Go to **2**.

117

'Let's start with the easy ones first,' suggests Bob. 'The third group tend to be medium to large companies with small invoice amounts – they know that we have the money and are likely to be patient if we don't overstretch the delay in payment. That will save about £55 000 over the next month. Shall I delay paying them until after the deadline?'

What is your response?

(a)   Yes, let Bob pay them on the first Monday after the deadline. Go to **205**.

(b)   No, pay them as usual and move on to the next group of suppliers. Go to **231**.

118

As you might expect, Essayess work on the principle that the due date for payment is the date on which to send the cheque – which they do.

Unfortunately it arrives too late for you to include it in your cash flow target. A missed opportunity!

Score: Essayess £nil; Business Points −1. Go to **201**.

119

The second item is Eggy Limited which owes £45 000, two weeks overdue. Shirley admits that she has not chased this account and offers to do so now while you are here. Do you want her to

(a)   ring Eggy now? Go to **191**.

(b)   check the file on Eggy first? Go to **240**.

120

Shirley now gets the file for ToyBoyz Limited. They owe £220 000, more than three months overdue. Shirley has notes of the stream of excuses that have been offered in the past:

- They have not received the invoice (Shirley sent a copy).
- They needed proof of delivery (they bought a six-foot-wide Sorter/Developer, but Shirley

sent a copy of the signed delivery note anyway).

- The computer is down (an excuse used four times!).
- There are no cheque signatories in the office this week (used twice).

Do you

(a)   wish Shirley luck with this one and leave it to her? Go to **43**.

(b)   ring ToyBoyz's Financial Director? Go to **172**.

(c)   tell Derek, your MD, that you may have a potential bad debt write-off coming up? Go to **81**.

(d)   tell Shirley to instruct the company's solicitors to commence legal recovery of the debt? Go to **39**.

121

Bob offers the following advice. 'There are certain things that we probably ought to pay, but it's up to you. First, VAT – the quarterly settlement is due right at the end of this month. It'll be for £400 000. Second, there's utilities – gas, electric, water and so on. We could probably stall for a month, since we normally pay these on time. It's unlikely that we'd be cut off within a month. The total for these is £110 000. Third, we owe our sister company, Ammag, £43 000, payable at the end of this week. The group instructions are specific: intercompany payments should be made on time.'

He continues, 'I assume that we'll pay salaries and wages and honour the direct debits set up at the bank for such items as lease rentals.'

You nod your agreement at his last point then review the three areas he suggests ought to be paid. He looks you straight in the eye and asks, 'Should I pay the VAT on time?'.

Your reply is:

(a) 'Yes, prepare it as normal and pay it.' Go to **223**.

(b) 'Yes, but is there any way in which we can reduce the amount to be paid?' Go to **108**.

(c) 'No, delay it until the week after the deadline. I'm sure the VAT people won't notice a few days' difference.' Go to **9**.

122

Having taken you through those three items, Bob raises the thorny question of your routine suppliers – companies that provide everyday products and services. Should he pay any of them over the next four weeks? Go to **29**.

123

As a result of a letter from your solicitors, the following week, Triller send a cheque for £392 000, but still refuse to pay the disputed £8000. They also cancel current orders for £950 000! This takes £240 000 out of the cash forecast, leaving you just £152 000 better off.

By being bullheaded instead of willing to find out more first, you've missed out on some cash and damaged customer goodwill.

Score: Triller +£152 000; Business Points −3. Go to **119**.

124

During the week, while waiting for Mr Adale's return, do you

(a)   leave the account on ice until Mr Adale returns? Go to **100**.

(b)   let Shirley ring ToyBoyz every day just in case Mr Adale comes back sooner than expected? Go to **35**.

(c)   inform your Managing Director of the problem? Go to **2**.

(d)   decide that the only way that you are going to get paid is to take recourse to legal action? Go to **39**.

125

Together you work through the Aged Debtors' listing, which tells you how much is outstanding for each customer and how long it is overdue or when it will be due for payment. Four items stand out and none of them is in Shirley's collection forecast.

1.   Triller Limited: £400 000 due two months ago.
2.   Eggy Limited: £45 000 two weeks overdue.
3.   Synbad Saylor: £166 000 due six weeks ago.
4.   ToyBoyz Limited: £220 000 due nearly four months ago.

You start with Triller. Go to **165**.

126

You report your results to the Group Financial Director and she is most appreciative. She is not sure how you did it (but she will find out!), and thanks to your efforts, and those of the other companies in the group, the acquisition goes ahead successfully. Go to **107**.

127

There goes some more money. Paying Mystery Metals makes you appear at best indecisive, at worst weak.

Score: Mystery Metals −£120 000; Business Points −1. Go to **77**.

128

You telephone Bob and ask him about Eggy's account. He tells you that there are invoices totalling £60 000, but they are not due for payment for another six weeks! Go to **111**.

129

Someone from the VAT office rings you on Monday morning, demanding to know where your payment is (Bob did say they were very hot on this and he was right).

You apologize and tell the caller that, while the absence of your Financial Controller who normally does the VAT return is no excuse, you have only just seen and signed the return. You promise payment today, knowing that it is already on its way. You receive a warning that any repetition may result in the company moving to monthly returns – a nasty threat indeed.

The incidence is followed by an official letter stating that if you default on the VAT payment again in the next twelve months, there will be an automatic interest penalty.

You were lucky to get away with that one. Go to **25**.

130

Essayess post the cheque on the due date and you received it just in time – more by luck then judgement though!

Score: Essayess +£19 800; Business Points nil. Go to **201**.

131

You telephone Mr Adale and ask him what happened.

'We borrowed to expand the business, but the sales volume hasn't grown as quickly as we'd planned. We know that the potential sales are there, but it's taking us longer than anticipated to realize them. You can see that we're still profitable, but cash is the problem. Until we get the sales and the money in from our investment in new production facilities, high stock levels and interest payments, we need support from key suppliers such as you. Give me a month.'

What do you say?

(a) 'OK, I'll take the risk.' Go to **26**.

(b) 'I'll have to check with my MD. I'll get back to you.' Go to **102**.

(c) 'No, sorry, I've my own problems. I need payment now.' Go to **147**.

132

This is a perfectly legitimate tactic, as long as the purchase invoices are all for deliveries made in the VAT quarter. All yours are.

Score: VAT +£8000; Business Points +2. Go to **25**.

133

For your second defence you have a choice. What is your response?

- (a) 'Can I speak to your Financial Director please?' (You want to reveal all about your cash flow target and solicit his or her help.) Go to **66**.

- (b) 'No, I'm afraid that I can't allow that. In fact we will not be paying you until the first Monday of next month. I can guarantee a cheque for you then – and you can certainly collect it.' Go to **207**.

- (c) 'OK, you win, I'll have a cheque ready for tomorrow.' Go to **127**.

134

Not only do Essayess send the cheque on the due date, it is posted first class and it is delivered in time. That is fortunate.

Score: Essayess £20 900; Business Points nil. Go to **201**.

135

Shirley does as you ask, then looks back at you. 'In that case, he'd like to speak to the Financial Director.'

Do you

(a) tell Shirley to say that she knows you are not in your office right now? Go to **4**.

(b) take the call? Go to **86**.

136

The Sales Director, Claire, is in and welcomes you into her office. You explain the issue at hand and she asks how she can help. You point out that cash flow is basically down to two things – getting money in and controlling it going out. You may need her cooperation in the first area. She asks if there is anything specific that you have in mind. Go to **249**.

137

Mr Adale tells you that you can threaten him all you like, but it is not the best way of getting paid. Then he hangs up.

Do you

(a)   ring him back? Go to **248**.

(b)   instruct your solicitors to commence legal action? Go to **39**.

(c)   leave it to Shirley from now on? Go to **43**.

138

'Thirty days are our standard credit terms, but I can try.' Claire rings Tinklebell's Production Manager. She points out that she has a Multiplexer in stock, but that it has been allocated to another customer. However, if he can convince his finance department to settle the account within 14 days instead of 30, she will reroute the product to Tinklebell instead. He promises to ring back shortly. Go to **229**.

139

'This final group are the ones that could be tricky,' explains Bob. 'If we don't pay these people within a couple of days of the due date, they are on to us in a flash. It will be very difficult for my people alone to deal with these suppliers. After our initial stalling tactics, they will want to go straight up the line to the Financial Controller – or while he is away, you. Mind you, not paying them will add £410 000 to the cash flow.'

Are you prepared to deal with a number of belligerent suppliers yourself? It may come to that if you do not pay this group. Do you decide to

(a) pay these suppliers without delay? Go to **104**.

(b) go for broke, and pay them after the dead-line – after all, you are the customer? Go to **243**.

140

Bob knows the suppliers better than you do. Listen to him. Go to **117**.

THE CASH FLOW CHALLENGE

141

Go to **12**.

142

You have gained a temporary advantage, but of course the despatch notes and their resulting invoices are entered in the following VAT quarter and you will end up paying for them in the next return. However, first you have to survive the VAT inspector's audit. Go to **162**.

143

Claire rings Essayess and talks to the Managing Director. She tries to persuade him to accept immediate delivery, but does not seem to be having much success. In the middle of the conversation she suddenly says, 'I will have to consult the Financial Director. Just one moment please.'

She explains to you that Essayess do not need immediate delivery but, for a 10 per cent discount on the price, will accept it. Claire thinks that the MD reckons that she is short of sales, not cash.

Do you

(a) tell Claire to tell the MD there's no deal? Go to **181**.

(b) agree to the 10 per cent discount? Go to **173**.

(c) agree to the 10 per cent discount only if Essayess pay cash on delivery? Go to **154**.

(d) ask Claire to knock him down to 5 per cent? Go to **188**.

(e) ask Claire to negotiate 5 per cent plus cash on delivery? Go to **224**.

144

Somewhat surprised at your request, Mr Adale gives you the name and number of his bank manager, Mr Andrews. You ring Mr Andrews straightaway and ask him

(a) 'Are ToyBoyz really expecting £500 000 from a foreign customer?' Go to **13**.

(b) 'What is ToyBoyz's financial position?' Go to **163**.

145

Dominic's reply is terse. 'I was trying to be helpful, but if that's your attitude, then I want full payment tomorrow or you are on stop.'

This is your last chance. Do you

(a) pay? Go to **127**.

(b) call his bluff? Go to **33**.

146

An idea strikes you out of the blue! You could sell and lease back some of your plant and machinery. Basically you would sell some of your assets and rent them back, although it would entail a longer term of financing than you currently require. Still, it might be worth a thought.

Do you

(a) forget it and move on to someone else who may be able to help? Go to **220**.

(b) ring the leasing company for more information? Go to **72**.

147

'I'm very sorry,' says Mr Adale, 'then I can't help you. I simply do not have the money right now. Goodbye.' He hangs up.

Do you

(a)   stop chasing this one for a month and see if ToyBoyz survives? Go to **26**.

(b)   recourse to legal action? Go to **84**.

(c)   tell your Managing Director? Go to **2**.

148

To omit the gory details, you receive a severe dressing down! Nobody supports your decisions which threaten production and sales 'just to achieve some arbitrary accounting number', to quote the Production Director.

It is not an enjoyable experience, but you do manage to keep your job, although you lose much of your co-directors' respect.

To add insult to injury, the MD also orders you to pay all suppliers on time, to avoid any repetition of this humiliating incident.

Score: erase all £ scores relating to suppliers

and creditors. Keep the Business Points you had and subtract −20 for this sorry episode. Go to **53**.

149

Although the MD is understanding, she points out that Mr Adale is handling this and that you will have to wait until his return. Go to **96**.

150

It is worth £100 to guarantee a payment of that size. Good thinking!

Score: Multiplexer +£34 900; Business Points +4. Go to **48**.

151

You were patient, but other suppliers were not. One insisted on being paid and initiated legal action. That prompted the bank to call in its debenture to protect its loan. Your company then joined the list of unsecured creditors as ToyBoyz was liquidated. You might feel unlucky, but there might have been ways and means to rescue something out of the situation.

Score: ToyBoyz £nil; Business Points −2. Go to **43**.

152

Claire explains the position. 'We have one Whizzo Multiplexer in stock – the basic model. It will take three months to build another, which Louise has scheduled into production. I have two customers wanting this product: first, Tinklebell Limited, in Liverpool, which has placed an order worth £35 000 for the basic model and, second, Hajid of India, which will pay £60 000 for a modified version, which is the basic model plus several accessories, all of which we have in stock.

'Because of our normal production lead times, both have indicated that they will accept delivery any time in the next three months. I had intended to sell it to Hajid and build the other one for Tinklebell. Is that all right by you?'

What is your response?

(a) 'Yes, go ahead – £60 000 is better than £35 000.' Go to **215**.

(b) 'Tell me more about the Hajid deal first.' Go to **198**.

153

The VAT is paid one working day late. It saves a large sum of money, but is a reprehensible action – you are opposing the government here.

Score: VAT +£400 000; Business Points –6.

What are the consequences of your action? Go to **129**.

154

The MD dithers for a while and then agrees. Claire sets the wheels in motion and, by the end of the week, you have the cheque. Decisive action has led to a positive result.

Score: Essayess +£19 800; Business Points +1. Go to **201**.

155

Barry agrees and will try to sort it out on his visit. Go to **209**.

156

The switchboard at ToyBoyz seems to be having trouble locating Mr Adale until you say that you are going to drive over to see him personally. Suddenly he is on the line – all sweetness and light. Firmly, and quite loudly, you tell him that the cheque has bounced.

'It must be a timing difference. Perhaps our incoming funds haven't cleared yet. I'll send you another one!'

Do you

(a)   accept another cheque? Go to **32**.

(b)   ask if his debtor has now paid? Go to **218**.

(c)   insist on a bank transfer today? Go to **242**.

157

It seems that Eggy Limited is not only a customer but also a supplier and, according to their invoice records, you owe them £60 000. They will not pay unless you do.

Do you

(a)   agree to let Shirley organize an exchange of payments? Go to **97**.

(b)   decide to leave this one? Go to **204**.

(c) check with Bob, the Purchase Ledger Supervisor? Go to **128**.

158

The following Monday, Mr Adale is due in his office. You telephone, and he is there. You remind him of your previous conversation.

'Yes, I remember. I think it's almost sorted out now.'

You insist that, if it is not, your Production Director will visit to put it right.

'I don't think the outstanding difficulties warrant that!' he exclaims.

You counter, 'Then I don't think they warrant any further delay in payment either!'

Mr Adale reluctantly agrees, but then changes tactics. Go to **34**.

159

They agree to your demand. Five days later you receive a cheque. Persistence does indeed have its rewards!

Score: Synbad +£166 000; Business Points +2. Go to **120**.

160

What an interesting and exciting month! What an experience! So how did you do? First of all, did you raise the £1 000 000? Go to **68**.

161

There is probably not a great deal of hesitation in your decision-making style – 'if they get in my way, tough luck!' However, you should remember that you have to carry on working with these people for the rest of your time in the job. Even if you achieved your target, the Group Financial Director (among others) may have a different moral stance. A boss will tolerate a 'go-for-it anyway' employee until that employee becomes a threat or a liability. Go to **256**.

162

VAT officers are not necessarily members of Mensa, but neither were they born yesterday. Checking the books of so many different companies each year gives them plenty of experience in spotting a more subtle sleight of hand than you have permitted to be carried out. You have been found out! Go to **113**.

163

Mr Andrews' response is 'I cannot divulge such information and I am surprised that you ask.' Go to **115**.

164

Tinklebell is a prompt payer and, on the due date, sends you a cheque for £35 000. However, even though it is posted first class, it does not reach you until the following Monday – just too late. You nearly got it right.

Score: Multiplexer £nil; Business Points +2. Go to **48**.

165

Shirley explains that Triller are disputing one of the invoices, claiming that the products received were damaged. Your warehouse manager is adamant that they left in good condition and that it is not his problem. Triller is refusing to pay unless your company sends a credit for the damaged goods which are valued at £8000. Do you

(a) authorize a credit note for £8000? Go to **54**.

(b) ring the warehouse manager? Go to **225**.

(c) ring Claire, the Sales Director? Go to **182**.

(d) ring Triller? Go to **41**.

(e) ring the solicitors to commence legal recovery of the debt? Go to **123**.

(f) leave this to Shirley? Go to **233**.

166

'No, I'm afraid not – a cheque requires two signatories.' She adds that she would not want to go behind Mr Adale's back if he is handling it. You will have to wait for his return. Go to **124**.

167

You tell the bank manager that the company is making some imminent investments in plant and machinery and that you need some funds to tide you over.

He then tells you that he knows about your Group's potential acquisition, because his bank has agreed to fund half of the money if the Group finds the rest. He puts down the telephone, angry at your dishonesty.

Score: Bank £nil; Business Points −1. Go to **146**.

168

Despite Shirley's calls, Essayess sent the cheque a couple of days late – they only pay suppliers once a week and the timing just fell wrongly for you. Close, but not close enough!

Score: Essayess £nil; Business Points nil. Go to **201**.

169

Bob looks decidedly uneasy about your decision. 'That could cause a few problems.'

You ask him to be more specific and he continues, 'I split the suppliers into three groups, basically according to their likelihood of creating difficulties. If you want, I can take you through each of the three groups, or would you still prefer not to pay any of them?'

Do you

(a)   change your mind and let Bob give you his supplier analysis? Go to **140**.

(b)   decide that non-payment might cause too many problems and decide to pay them all? Go to **189**.

(c)   stand fast and tell Bob not to pay anyone? Go to **238**.

170

Mr Adale responds smoothly: I agree and, technically, we are outside the terms of the contract, but we're only talking about minor hiccups with the machine, although they are losing us production and sales. It seemed an awful lot of trouble and expense to bring in your people for what appeared to be relatively simple tinkering, although I am not a technical man myself.'

'That is as maybe', you reply, 'but I'd feel happier if our technical people were helping you. The sooner the problems are resolved, the sooner you will be up and running trouble-free. In the meantime you can send me a cheque for £220 000 and I will arrange for top technical advice and any retraining that you feel is necessary.'

Mr Adale makes a counter-offer: 'Tell you what, give us until the end of the week. I will put pressure on the Production department to make sure everything is satisfactory by then and I can pay you in full. How does that sound?'

What is your response?

(a) 'OK, I'll leave it with you.' Go to **15**.

(b) 'No, if you have problems which are causing you not to pay, I am sending my team in. I insist!' Go to **73**.

171

Bob calls you. 'Onu Oils are on the line. They're coming up to their year end, so they want to get their debts in. It's for £18 000. Shall I pay them?'

(a) Yes. Go to **237**.

(b) No. Go to **78**.

172

When you ask for the Financial Director, the switchboard operator asks who is calling. You tell her and, after a few seconds, you are told that the Financial Director is in a meeting right now. Do you

(a) leave a message asking him to ring you back? Go to **60**.

(b) hang up and leave this one? Go to **43**.

(c) persist, saying that it is imperative that you speak to him to prevent imminent legal action? Go to **17**.

(d) say that you will hold the line for a while? Go to **255**.

173

The MD of Essayess accepts the 10 per cent discount. The order and delivery go ahead, priced at £19 800. The due date for payment is very close to your deadline and, as you realized earlier, you have no track record of how reliable Essayess is at paying. Nearer the due date, Shirley, the Credit Controller, rings to check that there are no potential problems and finds none.
Do you want to

(a) rely on the cheque turning up on time? Go to **250**.

(b) ask Shirley to ask Essayess if you can arrange for a courier to collect the cheque on the due date? Go to **16**.

174

The cheque arrives on the appointed day, so the results have justified your decisions.

Score: Multiplexer +£35 000; Business Points +3. Go to **48**.

175

Score: Ammag £nil; Business Points +1.

There is no point in scoring off your own companies – the whole group is trying to raise cash, not just move it from one part to another. Go to **122**.

176

'I've been in the same situation myself in the past, and I dare say I will be again sometime,' says Dominic. 'If you can promise me payment on that Monday, I will give you until then. We've been trading partners too long to lose goodwill over a few weeks. Good luck with the rest of it.'
    You did it!

Score: Mystery Metals £nil; Business Points +1. Go to 77.

177

It all goes through smoothly and you get the cheque. Positive action brings positive results.

Score: Essayess +£19 800; Business Points +1. Go to **201**.

178

The figures for Toyboyz are as follows:

	Statutory Accounts Last Year End £'000s	**Internal Accounts** Latest £'000s
Fixed assets	3 736	4 944
Current assets:		
Stocks	2 842	3 586
Debtors	1 409	1 685
Cash	140	(28)
Creditors due within one year	(3 587)	(5 574)

Net current assets	<u>804</u>	<u>(331)</u>
Total assets less current liabilities	4 540	4 613
Creditors due after more than one year:		
Bank loan	2 500	2 500
Others	80	78
Net assets	<u>1 960</u>	<u>2 035</u>
Capital and reserves:		
Share capital	100	100
Reserves:		
Profit	1 740	1 815
Revaluation	120	120
Total funds	<u>1 960</u>	<u>2 035</u>

Go to **131**.

179

Barry is very helpful. He tells you that Atled supply the grinding blades that fit your machine, as well as others that Synbad use. He has dealt with Synbad for several years and, indeed, he is going out to visit them in about six weeks' time. He doesn't know whether there is any problem with payments, but offers to transfer you to Jim, Atled's Credit Controller.

Jim tells you that Synbad are slow payers but, once they get a fax from his Financial Director asking for the money, payment follows soon after.

After thanking Jim for his help, do you

(a) ask him to put you through to his Financial Director to ask for his advice? Go to **219**.

(b) ask him to transfer you back to Barry? Go to **8**.

(c) hang up and ask Shirley to send a suitably worded fax to Synbad in your name (and title!). Go to **85**.

(d) decide that this is getting too complicated and leave it to Shirley from now on? Go to **120**.

180

You smile back, equally radiantly. 'I agree that the primary responsibility for cash collection falls within my domain and, indeed, you and your team often cooperate by occasionally contacting customers to discover the real problem. You even agree to stop further supplies if that's what it takes. What I mean is that a sale is not a sale until we get paid for it.'

Claire considers your point of view for a few seconds. 'Yes, you're right of course. However, in the first instance, Shirley will have all the relevant details. I'll help where I can with specific problems, as I've always done. In the meantime is there another way that I can help you?' Go to **249**.

181

Claire passes on the message and the MD hangs up. She cannot help you any more, so you return to your office. You were not prepared to trade profits for quick cash, no doubt because you are aware that other opportunities will arise.

Score: Essayess £nil; Business Points +1. Go to **201**.

182

You explain what you know to Claire. She was unaware of the problem and agrees that, because Triller is a very important customer, the best solution is to send them a credit note for the full

£8000. You tell Shirley to inform Triller that a credit note is on its way. Triller send a cheque by the end of the week.

A little work on your part has reaped dividends.

Score: Triller +£392 000; Business Points +2. Go to **119**.

183

'Five per cent? That's £1100, I suppose.' He is obviously weakening and Claire moves in for the kill. You can see why she is a good Sales Director – she can still do the selling too.

'That's right, £1100 off the price if you can accept immediate delivery. I know that one passed through Inspection yesterday, so it is all in perfect working order. I can also give you three months' warranty instead of the usual one month.' Claire covers the mouth-piece and whispers to you, 'Don't worry, a Model B Gantry system normally runs maintenance free for a year.'

The Managing Director at Essayess agrees the deal. Go to **103**.

184

You have now had the opportunity to speak to both the MD and the Production Director – the only Board member left is the Sales Director. Do you want to go and talk to her?

    (a)   Yes. Go to **136**.

    (b)   No. Go to **201**.

185

You have no trading experience with Essayess by which to judge whether or not they will pay on time. The cheque is due just before the final day for your cash target, so really you are relying upon them to send it on or before the due date.

    Will they? Choose

    (a)   Go to **118**.

    (b)   Go to **11**.

    (c)   Go to **203**.

    (d)   Go to **134**.

186

The Production Manager's response is vague. 'Oh, they're only small problems. We'll get them sorted out, there's no need to send your people. I'll keep Alan Adale informed when he gets back. Goodbye.'

Do you

    (a)   ring the MD of ToyBoyz? Go to **149**.

    (b)   wait for Mr Adale to return? Go to **96**.

    (c)   speak to your MD? Go to **116**.

187

'It's probably the biggest supplier of one of our major raw materials. That it is why the invoice is for so much.'

That does appear to put a different complexion on matters. Bob puts the call through to you. Go to **83**.

188

'Five per cent? Forget it!' You can hear the MD clearly from your side of the desk. 'You obviously need this sale more than I do. It's 10 per cent or I'll wait for delivery next month.'

Claire looks to you for an answer. Do you

   (a)   insist that 5 per cent is all that he is going to get? Go to **183**.

   (b)   agree to 10 per cent? Go to **173**.

   (c)   agree to 10 per cent if it is linked with cash on delivery? Go to **252**.

   (d)   really push it, sticking at 5 per cent plus cash on delivery? Go to **93**.

189

You've made an ethically sound decision. Your suppliers look to you to honour the credit terms, as you expect your customers to do the same. Just because you are sometimes paid late does not give you licence to abuse your creditors' position. However, you've added nothing to your cash flow.

Score: Suppliers £nil; Business Points +12. Go to **53**.

190

It did – ToyBoyz pulled through with the cooperation of key suppliers. The future is still uncertain, but with continued support, they are confident of eventual success. Anxious to secure supplies, after your deadline they pay you in full and even understand your decision to halve their credit limit. You have played a key role in their survival.

Score: ToyBoyz £nil; Business Points +5. Go to **43**.

191

Shirley rings Eggy Limited. As she enquires as to why they have not paid, you can hear an angry voice at the other end of the telephone. Shirley just listens with an occasional 'Oh, I see' and a 'I didn't know that'. Suddenly she looks at you and holds out the telephone. 'He wants to speak to the Financial Controller.'
Do you

(a) tell Shirley to inform whoever is on the other end of the line that the Financial Controller is on holiday? Go to **135**.

(b) take the telephone from her? Go to **86**.

192

You've made a sensible business decision, even though it doesn't produce any extra cash.

Score: Utilities £nil; Business Points +1. Go to 70.

193

You receive a cheque for £5000. Something is better than nothing, which is what you might have received otherwise.

Score: ToyBoyz +£5000; Business Points +1. Go to 43.

194

In real life you would be feeling quite low at this stage. Fortunately you can always have another go at this game and try to get a better result next time! Before you launch into another attempt, go to 107.

195

'Stocks? Yes, they are my responsibility – what do you want me to do?'

You ponder for a moment and then explain, 'Our stock level is forecast to rise by £80 000 over the next month. Although some of those supplies would not have been paid for by the end of the month, and so fall into the creditors' figures, the remainder will come out of cash flow – unless, of course, you can avoid buying it in the first place.'

Louise is defensive. 'Listen, I run production on pretty minimal stocks as it is.'

You nod your agreement. 'I realize that, but could you delay some deliveries until next month? Just defer the replenishment order for some of the bigger items?'

'OK, I could do that for some deliveries.' She borrows a pad from your desk and makes a few notes. 'I reckon that if I hold back these three lines, it would be worth about £100 000. As you would probably have paid half of that by the month end, you could work on a cash flow saving of, say, £50 000.'

Louise leaves to put her plan into operation. In the end the cash flow saving works out slightly better. If you hadn't asked for her help, you would have gained nothing.

Score: Stocks +£54 000; Business Points +2. Go to **184**.

196

Sure enough, a cheque arrives from ToyBoyz. You wait until Monday to bank it. Go to **57**.

197

Louise goes into a wealth of technical detail, but you gather that the machine gets through a high volume of quality blades and that, normally, she fits blades manufactured by your sister company, Atled.

Do you want to

(a)   ring Barry, the Sales Director at Atled? Go to **179**.

(b)   leave this and move on to another account? Go to **120**.

198

'Hajid are a regular customer, although this is a big item for them – well, it's a big item for anybody,' explains Claire. 'Because Hajid are an export customer, they get the standard 90 days' credit.'

You realize that this does not help you with your cash target. Do you ask Claire

(a) to give you the terms of Tinklebell's order? Go to **7**.

(b) if she could reduce Hajid's credit terms? Go to **99**.

199

By Wednesday you have heard nothing, so you telephone Mr Adale again. He tells you that the money should arrive in his bank tomorrow – surely you can bear with him for another 24 hours? Can you?

(a) Yes. Go to **91**.

(b) No. Go to **90**.

200

The Group Financial Director receives your results and is pleased that you came quite close to the target. She does not enquire too deeply as to how you raised so much in so short a time, since her first priority is to check whether the Group made its total target. Even though you are a little short of your given target, other performances in the Group (particularly the Financial Director at Ammag) make up the difference. The acquisition goes ahead successfully. Go to **107**.

201

It is time to start involving your own department. Your Financial Controller is on holiday so you will have to deal with his staff yourself. There are really only two people who can help you: Shirley, the Credit Controller, in charge of the team that encourages customers to pay on time and Bob, the Purchase Ledger Supervisor, whose team processes suppliers' invoices and prepares cheques to pay suppliers.

As Shirley's office is the nearest you decide to start with her. Go to **216**.

202

Go to **221**.

203

Nothing arrives from Essayess on the due date. Shirley telephones the following Monday, but it took a little pressure before they paid at the end of the week – too late for your deadline. This has been a case of doing too little too late.

Score: Essayess £nil; Business Points −1. Go to **201**.

204

You and Shirley begin to discuss the next account, Synbad Saylor Limited in Egypt, which shows a debt of £166 000 which is six weeks overdue. You ask her for more details. From the file, she tells you that Synbad bought a Hyper Deluxe Grinding machine on 30 days' credit. Synbad has not replied to any of her faxes asking if there is any reason for the failure to pay. She has also tried to telephone several times, but is never put through to anyone who can help. They promise to ring back, but have not yet done so.
Do you

(a)   leave this one to Shirley? Go to **120**.

(b)   look at their sales/payment history? Go to **63**.

(c)   ring Claire, the Sales Director to ask if she knows anything about Synbad? Go to **28**.

(d)   ring Louise, the Production Director, to ask what a Hyper Deluxe Grinding machine is? Go to **197**.

205

This course of action might be taking advantage, but it does help towards your cash flow. Of course, it will undoubtedly upset a number of people.

Score: 3rd   Creditors   +£55 000;   Business Points −3. Go to **52**.

206

No harm done. Go to **220**.

207

'You're an important customer to us', says Lucy, ('And don't I know it!' you think to yourself) 'but we are also an important supplier to you.'
   A thinly veiled threat! Do you

(a) concede and pay up? Go to **127**.

(b) refuse immediate payment and hope that the Purchasing Manager can quickly source the material from elsewhere? Go to **33**.

(c) ask her to spell it out for you? Go to **6**.

208

ToyBoyz tried and failed. The temporary cash flow problem quickly became a permanent one. Suppliers were reluctant to supply and the bank eventually lost patience. ToyBoyz was liquidated and the assets seized by the bank under the terms of a debenture securing its loan. You and the other unsecured creditors received nothing. The debt will have to be written off and you might wonder if only you had done something different at some stage. . . .

Score: ToyBoyz £nil; Business Points −3. Go to **43**.

209

Barry is away for two weeks, touring Middle East customers. On his return, he reports that Synbad have said that there are no problems, that they must have overlooked the matter and are very sorry. They promise to send a cheque within 30 days. They do so, but unfortunately this is long after your deadline.

Asking someone with more knowledge and experience for help is a good idea, although it didn't pay off this time.

Score: Synbad £nil; Business Points +1. Go to **120**.

210

'I can't think of another way to help you. I simply don't have that much money at the moment. You will have to accept a postdated cheque or nothing.' The cheque is better than nothing, so you take that. Go to **196**.

211

During the next month, and in particular the final two weeks, Bob's department comes under increasing pressure from individual suppliers. Morale flags a little, but the lure of the cheque run on the first Monday keeps the suppliers and the department to their purpose. It is not necessarily a pretty solution, but it does the job for you.

Score: 2nd Creditors +£260 000, Business Points −5. Go to **139**.

212

You explain to the MD that this is a one-off occurrence due to cash flow pressures from above. He is very understanding and promises to organize everything. Your diplomacy is rewarded.

Score: Essayess +£19 800, Business Points +1. Go to **177**.

213

'Debtors? That is between you and Sales, surely? I cannot help you there.'
Louise leaves. Go to **184**.

214

You have decided not to pay any utilities' bills for a month. Bob's team ignore the red payment demands that arrive in the third and fourth weeks of the month. Go to **87**.

215

Claire instructs the senior administrator to book the Multiplexer in stock to Hajid and invoice it. Sales increase by £60 000 and so do debtors. Since Hajid is getting 60 days' credit, the £60 000 stays in the debtors listing until well after your deadline. You chose profit over cash.

Score: Multiplexer £nil; Business Points nil. Go to **48**.

216

You explain the position to Shirley. She shows you her sales and collection forecast for the next month.

	Sales forecast	**Collection forecast**
	£'000s	£'000s
UK	1 660	1 642
Export	420	400
	2 080	2 042

UK sales are generally on 30 days' credit and export are on 90 days. She has no details of the expected sales by customer. You review the current debtor listing with her. Go to **125**.

217

You call in to see Bob. It is Bob who normally prepares the weekly cheque runs which are then approved by your absent Financial Controller. Cheques over £10 000 always have to be signed by either yourself or your Managing Director.

With a little over four weeks to improve your cash flow, you know that half of the equation is to limit the cash going out of the company. You explain the background of the situation to Bob. Go to **121**.

218

'No, apparently someone has made a right mess of it. The money is in the system somewhere and it should turn up any day. Can I send you another cheque?'

What is your response?

(a) 'Yes.' Go to **32**.

(b) 'No. I want a bank transfer payment made today.' Go to **242**.

(c) 'Give me your bank manager's telephone number.' Go to **144**.

219

Michael, the Financial Director at Atled, under-stands your problem: he has been contacted by the Group Financial Director too. He tells you that Atled's dealings with Synbad tend to be worth about £5000 a time and that Synbad usually wait until he personally sends a fax to them before they pay. Now that he knows the rules, he sends the fax soon after the due date. However, he thinks that £166 000 is a much bigger debt than he has ever had with Synbad, but Barry could confirm that. He offers to transfer you back to Barry.

Do you

(a) accept? Go to **8**.

(b) thank him for his help, but decline, being sure that a fax from yourself will solve the problem. Go to **85**.

220

Just as you are considering who to approach next, Louise, the Production Director, walks past your office. How could she help with cash flow? Do you

(a)   call her in? Go to **94**.

(b)   let her continue on her way? Go to **184**.

221

Essayess turn out to be slow payers and it takes Shirley a few calls to secure payment – two weeks after your deadline. Could you have been more assertive in an effort to collect the money in time?

Score: Essayess £nil; Business Points −1. Go to **201**.

222

Go to **71**.

223

You do not really want to try it on with statutory bodies. This is a wise decision, at least from a legal point of view.

Score: VAT £nil; Business Points +2. Go to **25**.

224

'Don't be ridiculous, lassie!' storms the Essayess MD. Claire is outraged at being called 'lassie' in such a tone and tells him that a 5 per cent discount represents a £1100 saving to his company, and that this 'lassie' is offering him a good deal if only he could see it. You visibly wince and Claire recovers herself. 'Which I am sure you can,' she adds smoothly.

The MD does not quite see it in the same light. 'I don't agree. For cash on delivery and immediate acceptance of the goods, I want 10 per cent. Take it or leave it.'

Claire offers you the choice. Do you

(a)   take it? Go to **18**.

(b)   leave it? Go to **181**.

225

The warehouse manager maintains that the goods left your company in perfect condition. He also has a goods delivery note signed by Triller. The note has the standard printing 'Goods accepted in good order', but Triller has written over it 'Goods not checked'. Go to **254**.

226

'OK, I'll let you know if we get any problems,' says Bob. It is not long before he does – the next day in fact!

You've saved a considerable amount of money, but at what cost to both you and the company's reputation?

For the time being:

Score: 1st Creditors +£410 000, Business Points −7. Go to **171**.

227

Louise responds abruptly: 'I wasn't planning to make any capital expenditure for the rest of the year. I told John not to put anything in his cash forecast. I've no time for this – I've things to do', and she leaves. Go to **184**.

228

Bad news spreads quickly, although not everyone gets to hear it or takes notice of it. This has now become a damage limitation exercise.

Score: if you have a £ score for any of the

following, adjust as stated (but keep the Business Points for them):

- 1st Creditors – erase previous score
- Onu Oils – erase previous score
- Mystery Metals – erase previous score
- 2nd Creditors – if £nil, leave at £nil; otherwise adjust by −£140 000
- 3rd Creditors – if £nil, leave at £nil; otherwise adjust by −£15 000

and score a further Business Points −2. Go to **53**.

229

Two minutes later the Production Manager rings back, agreeing to the deal, as they need the Multiplexer straightaway. The order goes through and Tinklebell pay on time. Good negotiation and quick thinking has been rewarded.

Score: Multiplexer +£35 000, Business Points +5. Go to **48**.

230

There is another call from Bob later that day. 'Mystery Metals – we owe £120 000, due tomorrow. They were just checking that payment would be made. We tried stalling, but they want to pick up a cheque tomorrow. Shall I put them through to you?'

What is your response?

   (a)   'OK, give me the call.' Go to **83**.

   (b)   'Quick, tell me more about Mystery Metals!' Go to **187**.

   (c)   'Tell them that they can pick up the cheque tomorrow.' Go to **127**.

   (d)   'No, you handle it. Tell them what you like, but we are definitely not paying.' Go to **38**.

231

It is nice to see some old-fashioned respect for agreements between business parties.

Score: 3rd Creditors £nil; Business Points +3. Go to **52**.

232

Nothing is heard from Synbad during the next week, although Shirley has continued her efforts. Do you

- (a) ring Barry at Atled and ask him to raise the issue when he visits Synbad in five weeks' time? Go to **155**.

- (b) send a very strongly worded fax to Synbad? Go to **109**.

233

Shirley makes no further progress in the month because nobody will make a decision on the credit note.

Score: Triller £nil; Business points nil. Go to **119**.

234

'I'm sorry, but we just do not have the money at the moment,' admits Jennifer. 'We need a month to trade our way through.'

'OK, we've no option then. Thanks for being straight about it, Jennifer, and good luck,' declares Derek. 'All we can do is wait.' Go to **26**.

235

Mystery Metals collect a cheque for half of the debt. Console yourself with the thought that your honesty saved the other half!

Score: Mystery Metals −£60 000; Business Points +1. Go to 77.

236

It was a very good Friday for sales, although this course of action is simply defrauding HM Customs and Excise.

Score: VAT +£43 000, Business Points −10. Go to **142**.

237

You concede with as good grace as you can muster.

Score: Onu Oils −£18 000; Business Points −1. Go to **230**.

238

You've made a brave decision, but don't consider it as an easy option. Your decision will upset many people. In the meantime:

Score: Suppliers +£725 000; Business Points −9. Go to **171**.

239

How many days of despatch notes do you want to delay until the following week?

(a)   From today, a full 5 days? Go to **55**.

(b)   4 days? Go to **19**.

(c)   3 days? Go to **45**.

(d)   2 days? Go to **82**.

(e)   Just the last day? Go to **236**.

(f)   Or have you reconsidered the implications

and decided to process the extra purchase invoices only? Go to **132**.

240

The files show details of the outstanding invoices, the payment history for Eggy Limited (which usually pays a week late) and a note saying: 'Eggy is a supplier too. Check with Purchase Ledger first to make sure we are not overdue with them.'

You ring the Purchase Ledger Supervisor, Bob. He has invoices for £60 000, but they are not due for payment for another six weeks.

Armed with this information, Shirley succeeds in obtaining a cheque from Eggy. Finding that information proved worthwhile.

Score: Eggy +£45 000; Business Points +2. Go to **204**.

241

This action is sufficient to restore some confidence in your company, although there are lingering doubts over your performance.

Score: Erase all previous £ scores for:

- 1st Creditors
- Onu Oils
- Mystery Metals

or if you had a score for Suppliers, reduce it by £410 000. Score Business Points −3 (keeping your Business Points scores for the above). Go to 53.

242

There is a sudden silence on the telephone. Mr Adale clears his throat and suddenly sounds subdued. 'Look, let me be honest with you. I have a temporary cash flow problem and I need your help to get me through it. If I can defer paying you and other important suppliers for another month, I believe that we can trade our way through. Will you help?'

(a) No, you want to be paid now. Go to **251**.

(b) Perhaps. You ask for more information. Go to **74**.

243

Bob looks worried at your decision and you ask him why.

'It's not just the hassle it creates, because most of the suppliers in this category get paid relatively large amounts. The trouble is that most of them are also key suppliers. If the wrong supplier put a stop on deliveries at the wrong time, and we run out of an important material or component, it could close down production.'

'Good point, Bob,' you reply. Is it time to reconsider? Do you

- (a) decide that it would be best to pay this group after all? Go to **42**.

- (b) cross that bridge when you come to it. If a supplier does threaten to put you on stop, you can pay them – and only them – at that point. Go to **226**.

244

The cheque from Toyboyz bounces again. Do you

- (a) ring Mr Adale? Go to **156**.

- (b) tell your MD? Go to **2**.

(c)   chalk this up to experience and move on to someone who might pay? Go to **80**.

245

'Before you put the sale through, Claire, just let me check Tinklebell's payment record.'

You borrow her telephone to call Shirley, who tells you that Tinklebell is usually a prompt payer, invariably settling within seven days of the due date. Do you

(a)   let Claire sell the Multiplexer to Tinklebell? Go to **92**.

(b)   ask Claire if she could reduce Tinklebell's credit terms? Go to **138**.

246

'Fair enough,' he says. 'I'm just waiting for one of my major customers to pay me over £500 000 at the end of next week. I'll use that to settle with you. Is that all right?'

(a)   Yes. Go to **67**.

(b)   No. Go to **69**.

247

Barry can do this. He will threaten to cut off Synbad's supplies of grinding blades until they pay your company. Fortunately a delivery is due next week. Barry faxes Synbad, proposing delaying delivery unless they resolve your debt. They agree to pay and a week later you get a cheque for the full amount.

Having and using the right information has led to the right result.

Score: Synbad £166 000; Business Points +2. Go to **120**.

248

The receptionist says that Mr Adale is refusing to accept your call and that there is nothing that she can do.

Do you

(a) instruct the solicitors to commence legal action? Go to **39**.

(b) leave this for Shirley to chase? Go to **43**.

(c) put your MD in the picture? Go to **81**.

249

Do you elaborate on

    (a)   sales orders? Go to **31**.

    (b)   outstanding debtors? Go to **21**.

Or do you find that

    (c)   nothing comes to mind and leave her office? Go to **201**.

250

You are taking a risk. Even good payers rarely send their cheques to arrive at their suppliers on the due date – that is usually the earliest date when they will send it. Will Essayess get the cheque to you on time? Choose

    (a)   Go to **202**

    (b)   Go to **130**

    (c)   Go to **168**.

251

Mr Adale is almost pleading. 'We don't have the cash right now. You know that I must pay the statutory bodies, like VAT, tax and National Insurance, or else they'll wind us up, and then you'll lose everything. If I don't pay the wages, the workforce will leave and then we can't produce anything to earn money. If our major suppliers don't support us, we will go under and you will all lose. Will you reconsider and bear with us?'

Do you

(a)   refuse and insist on full payment now? Go to **147**.

(b)   agree because you see no alternative? Go to **26**.

252

Go to **154**.

253

Mr Adale calms down. You remind him of the size and age of the debt and list the stalling tactics that have been used by his company. Go to **246**.

254

So now you know. Do you

- (a) authorize a credit note for £8000? Go to **54**.

- (b) ring Claire, the Sales Director? Go to **182**.

- (c) ring the solicitors to start legal action? Go to **123**.

- (d) leave this to Shirley and move on to the next debtor? Go to **233**.

255

You are kept hanging on . . . and on . . . and on. Every few minutes, the receptionist repeats that the Financial Director is still in his meeting and he could be quite a while. It becomes apparent that he's not going to talk to you.
   Do you

- (a) leave a message asking him to ring you back? Go to **60**.

- (b) hang up and forget this one? Go to **43**.

- (c) tell her that you need to speak to the

Financial Director straight away to avoid possible legal action? Go to **17**.

256

You have reached the end of the task. You know how close you came to meeting the cash flow target and whether your business style is 'nice' or 'nasty'. Take a look at an appraisal of your overall performance and, having learned from the experience, try again!

Final Appraisal Grid

Cash Flow	Business Points		
	25 or more	6 to 24	5 or less
£900 000 or more	Promotion is surely imminent	Potential Group FD	Strong suspicion you would sell your Granny!
£700 000 to £900 000	Potential Group FD	Likeable all-round good character	You would sell your Granny, but not get the best price for her.

continued overleaf

£300 000 to £700 000	Replace a little idealism with pragmatism	Perhaps you were just unlucky this time	Go and buy some integrity and honesty
£300 000 or less	You are just too nice to be of any use	Change career while you still have some reputation	Useless and immoral – resign before you are fired

A Guide to Good Cash Flow Control

The following pages list a number of principles and practices which encourage the good management of cash flow.

You may wish to examine these ideas before you attempt to raise the funds for Daisy House plc, or perhaps after you have had a number of attempts.

Good cash management

Dealing with debtors

1. To avoid bad debts, don't sell to people who won't pay. Make sure that the customer agrees with the credit terms and be alert to such ploys as 'We only do one cheque run a month'.
2. The shorter the credit terms, the sooner you are entitled to receive the money. There is a balance between the profit on sale and how

much is lost in the way of interest due to extended credit terms. It is easy to sell to anyone if they don't have to pay for it!

3. One way of encouraging customers to pay before they are obliged to – that is, before the proper due date – is to offer a discount for payment for early settlement. Again, you should balance the advantage of the cash being received earlier against the cost of obtaining it.

4. Make sure that the invoices sent out are correct. If there is a pricing or quantity error in it, it is a golden opportunity for the customer to reject it and delay payment. In all likelihood, they won't even tell you it's wrong when they first get it, they will wait until you start to chase for payment.

5. As with so much else in life, if you don't ask, you don't get. Don't be shy about contacting the customer and requesting that the bills be paid. Ideally make contact a couple of days before payment is due to ensure that there are no barriers to payment.

6. When you ring, make sure that you speak to the person with the authority to make the decision to pay you. Otherwise all you've done is left a message that you would like to be paid.

7. You may need to ask more than once – persistence pays off.

8. You cannot bank or spend a cheque that's 'in the post'. Transfers directly to your bank account are much more reliable and quicker than cheques sent to you.

9. Politeness costs nothing. There is no point in getting agitated with a reluctant payer because, when it comes down to it, you need them to get the cheque raised, signed and posted. Antagonizing someone will not put them on your side, so be polite but firm and insistent.

10. The relationship between you and your customers is the same as between your suppliers and you – act accordingly.

11. Common excuses for non-payment are:

   - 'We haven't received the invoice' (fax a copy to them)
   - 'We need a signed proof of delivery' (fax that too)
   - 'None of the cheque signatories are in the office' (get confirmation of when they will be in; if you suspect a little dishonesty, find out their names and ring back to speak to them later)
   - 'The computer has broken down' (most companies can write a cheque out by hand if they have to)
   - 'The cheque's in the post' (ask how much is it for, what was the cheque

number and when was it posted, give them a couple of days' grace and ring back if it hasn't arrived)

12. It can help to use your salespeople to put pressure on the customer. Some will be wiling to help; some don't like to risk offending! Be aware that it is not the customer's Buying department that usually prevents payment, but Accounts. Even so the buyers may have some influence.

13. Escalate the pressure if matters don't progress. Tactics vary, from calling higher echelons of management to ask why payment hasn't been made, to putting further deliveries on stop, to threatening legal action, to actually suing the customer if need be.

Dealing with creditors

1. Longer credit terms mean that you don't have to pay until later.

2. Suppliers who are also customers may wish to 'contra' (offset the balances) amounts. You may too.

3. Creditors are not your bankers and, in an ideal world, should be treated as you would want your debtors to treat you.

4. VAT payable is the sum of output tax (VAT

on your sales invoices) less the sum of input tax (VAT on your purchases).

5. Honesty (sometimes) pays – if you haven't got the money to pay someone, you could try telling them when they can expect to get paid.

6. Prioritize payments if there is a limited amount of cash available.

7. Know the timing and size of unavoidable payments and work round them.

8. If the company doesn't spend it, you don't have to pay for it. The easiest way to avoid having creditors is not to buy something in the first place.

9. Never take anything personally!

General

1. Your Sales/Buying departments will know more about your customers/suppliers than you do.

2. Be honest and act with integrity.

3. Be firm and decisive when needed.

Challenge Score Sheet

Activity	£	Business Points
Total		

The Bottom Line

Practical Financial Knowledge for Managers

A Gower Novel

Alan Warner

In this remarkable book Alan Warner uses the power of romantic
fiction to explain the key concepts of business finance. By creating a
believable set of characters and a compelling story he has provided an
easy and enjoyable way to understand balance sheets, budgeting,
marginal costing, investment appraisal, profit maximization,
performance measurement and other modern accounting
techniques.

The story concerns Phil Moorley, Sales and Marketing Director of
Lawrence & Sons, and his relationship with Christine Goodhart, the
management accountant imposed on the company by its
conglomerate owners. Moorley's big professional weakness is his lack
of financial knowledge, but with Chris' help he begins to learn - and
the reader learns with him. In the process his feelings for Chris grow
stronger - but will she ever be willing to offer him more than
friendship and tutorials? After a number of crises, Moorley begins to
prepare himself for a more ambitious role. Then fate steps in, and
both his business and personal life take a swift new turn.

The Bottom Line is as far from a conventional textbook as can be
imagined. Its readability and its business setting combine to make it
the best possible introduction to business finance for the
non-accountant.

Gower

The Business Plan - Approved!

G Nigel Cohen

The Business Plan - Approved! is a comprehensive guide to creating an impressive and achievable business plan to win the approval of your bank manager and investors. It will help you to evaluate the business from the viewpoints of sales, costs, and cash and assimilate the information into a clearly defined business strategy. Written in a clear, down-to-earth style, with no technical jargon, it encourages you to see your business plan as a potential investor in the company would, answering some basic but crucial questions along the way • What is a business plan and why do we need one? • How do we go about creating a successful business plan? • What do banks and investors look for?

All aspects of the business plan are dealt with, from initial planning in order to decide which direction the business should follow, through to presenting the plan in a professional and persuasive document. Guidance is also provided on how to set the plan out in the style that bankers and investors expect to see.

Written by accountants with many years' experience of getting plans approved and vetting them for banks and investors, uniquely this book also includes the expert opinions of investors and lawyers themselves describing what makes them accept or reject a business plan. Two real life examples are provided as models and to focus the reader on common pitfalls.

The practical, no-nonsense guidance of *The Business Plan - Approved!* will be welcomed by anyone planning to grow a business, start up on their own, or, as a manager, justify their budget for the coming year.

Gower

The Essentials of Project Management

Dennis Lock

Project management skills are no longer just required by project managers, but by most of us in the natural course of our working lives. *The Essentials of Project Management* is a practical primer drawn from Dennis Lock's comprehensive and highly regarded textbook *Project Management,* which is now in its Sixth Edition and has sold tens of thousands of copies. In order to specifically answer the needs of the non-specialist, the content has been carefully selected and organized to form an accessible introduction to the subject.

The result is a concise but well-rounded account of project management techniques, concentrating on the key tasks of project definition, organization, estimating, planning and control, and paying special attention to the role of purchasing. With the aid of examples and illustrations, the book describes the essential project management procedures and explains how and when they should be used.

This is an ideal introduction for anyone for whom project management is part of their professional role (or who would like it to be), or for students for whom it is a component within a broader course.

Gower

How to Make More Profit

Michael K Lawson

What determines the profitability of your business? How can you identify the critical factors and turn them to your advantage? These questions lie at the heart of Michael Lawson's book.

Using a model based on the experience of more than 300 companies he examines the three groups of factors that influence the success of any business: the external environment, the communication process and the business process. These three areas are intimately linked, so that changes in any one of them will affect the others. Practical and down-to-earth throughout, the book shows you how to pinpoint the key profit-related problems - and what to do about them. Whether you are responsible for a complete business or just one unit or function, whether you work in a large company or a small one, *How to Make More Profit* will enable you to do just that.

Gower

It's Not Luck

A Gower Novel

Eliyahu M Goldratt

Alex Rogo has had a great year, he was promoted to executive
vice-president of UniCo with the responsibility for three recently
acquired companies. His team of former and new associates is in place
and the future looks secure and exciting. But then there is a shift of
policy at the board level. Cash is needed and Alex's companies are to
be put on the block. Alex faces a cruel dilemma. If he successfully
completes the turnaround of his companies, they can be sold for the
maximum return, but if he fails, the companies will be closed down.
Either way, Alex and his team will be out of a job. It looks like a
lose-lose situation. And as if he doesn't have enough to deal with, his
two children have become teenagers!

As Alex grapples with problems at work and at home, we begin to
understand the full scope of Eli Goldratt's powerful techniques, first
presented in *The Goal* the million copy best-seller that has already
transformed management thinking throughout the Western world.
It's Not Luck reveals more of the Thinking Processes, and moves
beyond *The Goal* by showing how to apply them on a comprehensive
scale.

This book will challenge you to change the way you think and prove
to you that it's not luck that makes startling improvements
achievable in your life.

Gower

The Meaning of Company Accounts

Sixth Edition

Walter Reid and D R Myddelton

The Meaning of Company Accounts first appeared in 1971 and quickly achieved recognition among managers, financial and non-financial alike. Its 'workbook' approach stems from the need for a treatment of financial accounting practice which readers at differing levels of knowledge can tailor individually to their learning requirements. The authors, both of them distinguished teachers of finance and accounting, adopt programmed learning techniques within a firmly structured text in order to provide for a wide variety of readers' needs. At controlled points the reader is invited to work through examples and write into the workbook his or her solutions to problems. These active responses both reinforce what has been learned and extend the reader's experience and skill in using, preparing and interpreting company accounts.

For this sixth edition, the authors have revised their text throughout to reflect recent developments and have included new examples for the reader to work through. The appendix of photocopiable formats covering financial ratios, segment analysis and cash/funds flow have been retained from the fifth edition.

Gower

The Problem Buster's Guide

Mike Allison

The Problem Buster's Guide is exactly what its title suggests. In
non-technical language, and using examples from a wide range of
businesses and from everyday life, it shows how problems can be not
just solved but turned into opportunities for improvement. In
showing how to tackle problems large and small, Mike Allison
describes more than thirty different problem-solving techniques and
explains how to select the most suitable for your problem.

Mike Allison sums up his book as 'the "Swiss Army Knife" of problem
solving books'. His refreshing approach will appeal to managers in all
types of organization.

Gower